Do You Have LACK?

Do You Have LACK?

Listening
Accountability
Credibility
Knowledge

*These qualities are needed in the workplace
and in ones personal life.*

Scott W. Godfrey

iUniverse, Inc.
New York Lincoln Shanghai

Do You Have LACK?

Listening Accountability Credibility Knowledge

iUniverse books may be ordered through booksellers or by contacting:

iUniverse
2021 Pine Lake Road, Suite 100
Lincoln, NE 68512
www.iuniverse.com
1-800-Authors (1-800-288-4677)

Because of the dynamic nature of the Internet, any Web addresses or links contained in this book may have changed since publication and may no longer be valid.

The views expressed in this work are solely those of the author and do not necessarily reflect the views of the publisher, and the publisher hereby disclaims any responsibility for them.

ISBN: 978-0-595-48064-7 (pbk)
ISBN: 978-0-595-60161-5 (ebk)

Printed in the United States of America

Foreword

For the past 30 years, I have noticed many changes in the workplace, which has affected people's lives and attitudes at work and in their personal life. I have determined that attitudes, philosophy and job related standards are not being set at the workplace. If a business does not have high standards for their employees and if those standards are not being followed this can deteriorate and in time dismantle a business.

If employees are not being taught company standards they are being set up to fail instead of being set up to accomplish their responsibilities. When an employees responsibilities are accomplished they will gain a sense of accomplishment and it will help customer satisfaction. When a person has a sense of accomplishment they will enjoy their job and that enjoyment will blend into their personal life. I can remember a couple of years ago someone told me to leave my problems at the office at the end of the workday; that way I would not take the problems home with me. For some people this will probably work; others could try to put that into practice, but some will keep on letting their work affect every area of their life.

This book will help you understand what changes need to take place in a person's attitude, work ethics and personal life. When these suggestions are implicated into ones daily life there will be results. I have worked with a number of people on repairing problems in their career and personal life and have seen positive results.

Some individuals will try to get others that are in that person's life or at their workplace accept their business tactics by bulling, rudeness, lying, over promising and under delivering. When a person does not assume accountability or responsibility for their actions they are forgetting that their daily responsibilities

vi   Do You Have LACK?

are to be accomplished to company standards. They will finally understand that they are responsible for their actions when they are reprimanded by management. When a person conducts him or herself in this manner, it will only lead to dissatisfied clients, potential clients, friends or family members.

I have seen many occasions where individuals working in their job positions were never trained properly, or were never held accountable for their actions. We need to understand we are responsible for our behavior and our actions. I believe that nobody gets up in the morning and asks, "What can I foul up today?" It comes down being taught differently or even trained in different work related areas they would succeed, and have a sense of accomplishment at their place of employment which would lead into a more positive attitude. They would also reap the benefits in their personal life with family members and friends.

This is I why I created LACK. These topics are needed at the workplace and in ones personal life. I have experienced first hand by putting LACK into my life and others personal life. By taking someone, where ever they are in life, and applying these topics at the workplace or personal life, they will see POSITIVE RESULTS. LACK can be used to help show someone that a change is necessary in their personal life or at their workplace. When a change takes place at their place of employment, those in their personal life will benefit by that needed change. For example; if you are driving and all of a sudden you approach a person who is flagging traffic to detour them from the road-works, that flag person is warning you not to go in that direction due to the road-work. In the same manner, these topics will be used to flag that person towards a better understanding of what is change is needed in their personal life as well as their career.

There are so many companies that send surveys to the consumers, such as products they have purchased, automobiles, homes, motorcycles, meals at restaurants, to services that were needed by the consumer. Those products or services are rated and once they are rated everyone will know if they did or did not meet the consumer's expectations. When they tally all of the information that was received by the consumer, then they will have an official rating for that manufacturer of goods and services. As a result, manufactures will know where they are at with today's consumer.

With LACK I changed the above rating method, with the reader rating themselves. When you read each page you need to determine if you have this quality or if you need to inherit this quality. For the ones who cannot answer questions honestly about their personal qualities, they will need to ask someone who they trust and will give them an honest answer about their qualities. If you have this quality you need to ask yourself if you need to fine tune that quality. If you do not have that quality you will understand what change is needed. Now, we have to remember there are no shortcuts to LACK. Grasping these qualities depends on the one who participates; and one needs to remember, the more you have LACK the more you will gain in your career and personal life.

In most cases a person's career affects their personal life as much as their personal life can affect their career. LACK can help you have a better outlook in the workplace, by understanding how to work with difficult customers. This can have a positive affect on productivity and revenue increases, which could lead to monetary increases.

Individuals are not so inclined to find another place of employment when they are trained and have the knowledge on how to conduct their day to day responsibilities. When this happens their personal life is not being centered and dwelling on the negativity that is at the workplace.

This positive change could take place once the need is recognized and then that change is applied. You have to understand that the change takes time to be formed in your daily habit. When you recognize that a change is needed and the change is applied, you will start striving toward the goal of LACK.

In 1983, I came up with a quote "Not Knowing is Worst than Knowing." When someone notices that you need one of the attributes of LACK, you need to examine yourself before you answer them back; they could have noticed a need in your life and recognize that a change could help you in your personal life and in your career.

After this forward there is a Personal Awareness Form that will help you identify any area(s) in your career and personal life that needs to be improved. You must answer every question on this form. If you cannot answer these questions honestly you need to ask a family member, personal friend or coworker to help you answer honestly. Only allow people you trust to help you.

LACK is defined in the following topics:

L is defined as Listening

A is defined as being Accountable

C is defined as Credibility

K is defined as Knowledge

Listening, accountability, credibility and knowledge are what individuals should have to succeed in business, and help them to have an abundant personal life. It is a proven factor that if an individual enjoys their place of employment, their personal life and their relationships outside the workplace will be more positive. I designed LACK to help everyone who puts these practices in place to have a more fulfilling life, on the personal side and at their place of employment. For example: if an individual works eight to nine hours a day, if you add one hour for lunch and at least one hour for the commute to the place of employment, that is an average of 11 hours a day used for your daily employment routine. If the average person sleeps for eight hours a night, there will be an average of five hours a day to call their own. If they have a family and they have to pick-up their children at day-care and run errands, it will decrease that time down to about three to four hours for yourself or for your family. If you are single your time frame for yourself could be even more demanding than a person who has a family because all your responsibilities will have to be accomplished by you.

Now ask yourself, where do you spend most of your time during the week? Most people will answer, work. That is where you spend most of your time, and how your day goes will have an outcome on your attitude and how you treat others. LACK will help you develop ways to change your thought process and how to work and communicate with people, whether they are difficult or not. Also, it will help you change a client's negative attitude into a positive attitude, gaining that client for life.

There is a page at the end of each chapter on Body Language. This will help you understand what a person is saying by the movements and gestures they are making before they even say a word.

Having a business these days' means being totally customer service orientated, as well as having a product that is in high demand. By having associates that are employed by a company, knowing how to overcome obstacles; including production, time and clients will make them have a sense of accomplishment at work. They also need to know how to assist a customer who is dissatisfied. By changing their view and resulting in a customer who is telling their friends about the great service they have received.

When reading LACK you need to take your time and ask yourself how you can apply this to your daily responsibilities, both at work and in your personal life.

When this is applied to your daily life, you will begin to see changes in your attitude toward others. Remember what the Golden Rule is! <u>Do onto others as you want others to do on to you</u>. Everyone wants to be treated fairly and honestly, and the more you put LACK into practice on a daily basis, your place of business will start reaping the benefits from customer satisfaction and you will see the positive results in your personal life. After you complete the questions on the Personal Awareness Form; there are the four main Topics of LACK.

Under each of the four main topics there will be adjoining topics that apply to the main topic. You will want to take a few minutes to mentally digest these words and their meaning. It would be best if you read and worked through one page every two days. It will take two days to start adding this to your daily routine. Remember, after 21 days it will become a habit.

The next part in LACK will be to answer a couple of questions.
The first question is what is the date you started to apply that needed quality?
The second question is what personally has to happen for a change to occur? This will let you know what you need start doing to obtain this quality.
The third question is, two weeks after the change has occurred, what has happened at the workplace and in your personal life? This is something that will help you understand when you add a positive quality to your life people's attitude will change towards you for the better. These qualities are there to help you live a more abundant life at the workplace, personal life and home life.

At the end there will be quote, read it and see how it could apply to your life.

There will be enough space on each page for you to write down the answers to these questions; or if you need more there will be two pages for notes at the end of each chapter. In the back of the book, for your personal information, write down the date and what positive effects this has had on you and others. There are many topics in this book that can help you raise the bar professionally and personally.

Let's get started.

Personal Awareness Form

Answer the questions below using the following:

Excellent: If there is not any problem in that area
Good: Very few problems in that area
Average: Some difficulty in that area
Below Average: Great difficulty in that area

1. When a person is talking to you, either at the workplace or in your personal life, you listen and pay attention to what they are saying?

    Excellent
    Good
    Average
    Below Average

2. How organized are you when you are starting a task or project at the workplace or in your personal life?

    Excellent
    Good
    Average
    Below Average

3. Do you achieve closure on your tasks, assignments or correspondence with people at the workplace?

    Excellent
    Good
    Average
    Below Average

4. Are you committed at the workplace and in your personal life?

    Excellent
    Good

Average
Below Average

5. Do you follow through at the workplace and in your personal life?

Excellent
Good
Average
Below Average

6. Do you demonstrate accountability at the workplace and in your personal life?

Excellent
Good
Average
Below Average

7. Do you show loyalty to others at the workplace and in your personal life?

Excellent
Good
Average
Below Average

8. Do you have a balance between the workplace and your personal life?

Excellent
Good
Average
Below Average

9. Are you reliable at the workplace and in your personal life?

Excellent
Good
Average
Below Average

10. Are you honest with your coworkers and friends?

Excellent
Good

Average
Below Average

11. Do you have a positive attitude at the workplace and in your personal life?

Excellent
Good
Average
Below Average

12. Are you efficient at the workplace and in your personal life?

Excellent
Good
Average
Below Average

13. Do you have credibility with others at the workplace and in your personal life?

Excellent
Good
Average
Below Average

14. Do you stay focused at the workplace and in your personal life?

Excellent
Good
Average
Below Average

15. Do you have knowledge about your responsibilities at the workplace and in your personal life?

Excellent
Good
Average
Below Average

16. Are you enthusiastic about your position at your workplace or about your personal life?

   Excellent
   Good
   Average
   Below Average

17. Do you show stability at the workplace and in your personal life?

   Excellent
   Good
   Average
   Below Average

18. Do you respect others in leadership or others in general at the workplace and in personal life?

   Excellent
   Good
   Average
   Below Average

19. How do you communicate when a problem occurs at the workplace or in your life?

   Excellent
   Good
   Average
   Below Average

20. Do you try to succeed at the workplace and in your personal life?

   Excellent
   Good
   Average
   Below Average

21. Do you take pride in your work and in your personal accomplishments?

   Excellent
   Good

Average
Below Average

22. Do you understand the process at your workplace?

Excellent
Good
Average
Below Average

23. How do you cope when circumstances change at the workplace and/or in your personal life?

Excellent
Good
Average
Below Average

24. Are you confident at the workplace and in your personal life?

Excellent
Good
Average
Below Average

25. How accurate do you try to be at work and in your personal life?

Excellent
Good
Average
Below Average

26. How do you handle difficult situations at the workplace and in your personal life?

Excellent
Good
Average
Below Average

27. How are your time management skills at work and in your personal life?

    Excellent
    Good
    Average
    Below Average

28. How do you handle circumstances beyond your control at the workplace and in your personal life?

    Excellent
    Good
    Average
    Below Average

29. Do you produce quality in your work and in your personal life?

    Excellent
    Good
    Average
    Below Average

30. Do you set expectations that can be achieved at the workplace or in your personal life?

    Excellent
    Good
    Average
    Below Average

31. How is your attitude at the workplace and in your personal life?

    Excellent
    Good
    Average
    Below
    Average

32. How would you rate your behavior at the workplace or in your personal life?

    Excellent
    Good

Average
Below Average

33. What kind of reputation do you have at the workplace and in your personal life?

Excellent
Good
Average
Below Average

34. Are you factual when you describe events at the workplace and in your personal life?

Excellent
Good
Average
Below Average

35. Do you show empathy, passion, gratitude, and concern at the workplace and in your personal life?

Excellent
Good
Average
Below Average

36. How believable are you at the workplace and in your personal life?

Excellent
Good
Average
Below Average

37. Do you have vision at the workplace and in your personal life?

Excellent
Good
Average
Below Average

38. Are you trustworthy and dependable at the workplace and in your personal life?

    Excellent
    Good
    Average
    Below Average

39. Do you show confidentially at the workplace and in your personal life?

    Excellent
    Good
    Average
    Below Average

40. Are you satisfied where you are in life or would you rather have career advancements and growth in your personal relationships?

    Excellent
    Good
    Average
    Below Average

The answer to these questions will help you to determine the areas that need to be improved in your career and personal life. By answering the questions honestly, and understanding what areas need improvement, this will help you move forward in your personal life and at your place of employment.

Excellent will indicate that a change is not needed.

Good will indicate that these traits are not an everyday practice of being used.

Average will indicate that these traits are being used when they benefit them in certain circumstances.

Below Average will indicate that these traits are not being used.

Personal Awareness Results

Write down the traits you wish to start working towards.

1.

2.

3.

4.

5.

6.

7.

Chapter 1

▼

Listening the L of
LACK

Listening: one who is paying attention during a conversation another person is giving.

Listening is one of the key factors in any relationship. It does not matter if it is in ones personal life, home life or the workplace: this quality can determine if you will receive promotions in your career or how relationships will progress.

This is a quality that not matter where you are in life, you need to acquire it. I cannot even tell you how many times I have heard from clients and workers that people do not want to listen to what others are saying. One would have to think that individuals would listen to what the other person is saying when it affects them. Listening is a lost ART and it is a shame that the ones who are not listing are stunting or severing those relationships.

When we are not listening to others we are indicating by our body language that we are not interested in what they are saying. Not listening to a client's needs will send them to your competition; or they will go to your employer and you could end up among the unemployed. I can remember when I was in management and I told someone who worked in my department that a particular issue had to be completed on a certain day. Before that date every week I would ask them how things were going and if they needed my help, then they would indicate to me that every thing is moving right along and almost completed. Before the issue, I asked them to tell me what had been done, and to my dismay, they were no further than when we first discussed the issue and the date it needed to be completed. So I asked them to tell me what I told them. It was not even close to what I had spoke to them about, so I referred to my notes and then I let them read my notes and they had a blank look on their face.

I asked to see their notes and compare with my notes and I proceeded to ask them what happened, they indicated to me that they were not paying attention. I wrote up a reprimand for that person, and they were demoted to another position. I discussed what had to be competed on this project to another person in my department, they took note on what was being discussed and told me they would get started on it right away. Before I could ask them what progress was being made on that project, they would approach me to let me know the progress. Because that associate listened, the project was completed one week ahead of schedule. Listening is one of the major keys to ones future career, personal and home life.

When meeting with a perspective client, I have found it best to clear your mind of everything that will cause you not to listen or pay attention. Also, carry a pad of paper and write down all the contact information and other information that will be needed to make that business transaction; this will help you to review later on.
In life I have found, that paying attention in most cases will indicate to the client, that you are being attentive to their message, which indicates you are listening and interested in what they are speaking to you about.

In this chapter the following pages have these corresponding topics under the main heading Listening:
Respect
Balance
Answer
Communication
Passion
Description
Emotion
Distracted
Gratitude
Repeat

Anticipate
Awareness
Body Language

It is not enough to do your best; you must know what to do, and THEN do your best.
W. Edwards Deming

<u>Respect</u>

Word: Respect
Word Definition: High regard, esteem

How you and others can benefit: By respecting a person on a personal level; including their religion, looks, background, sexual preference or whatever life has endured for them. We do not have to agree with a person's lifestyle, the way they live or what they believe in; but we need to show them respect. That should indicate to you that gossiping, back biting or even slander can lead to tarnishing a persons name and reputation.

Past experience about the word: I remember a couple of years ago when an associate at the workplace where I was employee started e-mailing false rumors about another associate. When false rumors are being spread about a person, that will plant seeds of doubt in to ones mind (the seed of doubt is when individuals forget all the good a person has done, and will only be dwelling on the bad that person was supposed to have done.) In this situation, the person that was being accused of wrong doing found out what was being said, went to their supervisor and told them about the rumor and proved to the supervisor that the rumor was false. The supervisor could see that they were being wrongly accused and went to the person who started the rumor and asked for their resignation. Apparently, that was not the first time the associate had done this to their coworkers.

Tips: It is sometimes better to keep things to yourself than to tarnish a person's reputation. Remember deceit will always make its way back around to the one who tries to get others to lose respect for another person.

Date for applying your change?

What personally has to happen for a change to occur?

Two weeks after the change occurred; what changes happened at the workplace and in your personal life?

The beginning of wisdom is to call things by their right names.
Chinese proverb

Balance

Word: Balance
Word Definition: The amounts of something being equal

How you and others can benefit: Balance is a part of life that all us of need to have, but it is a part that gets misunderstood. Your personal life and your place of employment have to have a balance. At the beginning of this book we indicated that a workday could consist of somewhere between nine and eleven hours. There will be times when you will have to finish that days work at home. When this is an everyday occurrence, you have to determine if your workload is too heavy for one person, or are you lacking in time management skills. If a person spends does not quality time with their family, it could lead to resentment from those in your personal life. When this is an everyday occurrence, this could cause a person to start disliking their job. When someone dislikes their job the quality of work will go down.

Past experience about the word: One of the greatest disservices that a person does at their place of employment and home is when they are not being honest that their workload is too heavy. I have found that it is in your best interest to be honest with your employer about the workload. I would ask if they have any helpful hints on how you can get your work completed at the workplace rather than take it home every night. Then maybe they will recognize that your workload is too much for one person. Before I would meet with my employer or supervisor, I would examine myself to make sure that I am giving them a day's work for a days pay.

Tips: I found out that if you do not respect your own time, whether it is at work or at home, others will not respect it either.

Date for applying your change?

What personally has to happen for a change to occur?

Two weeks after the change occurred; what changes happened at the workplace and in your personal life?

No person can be a great leader unless he takes genuine joy in the successes of those under him.
W. A. Nance

Answer

Word: Answer
Word Definition: Written or spoken reply

How you and others can benefit: When you are answering someone, at times it would be best if you send the answer in writing to back up the verbal reply. How it is said will also lead to how it is taken. If you say it with anger it could be followed up with anger. If it is said with respect, hopefully, it will be followed up with respect. Remember, in some cases you could be conducting business in the future with this person. It is better to be respectful than for someone to tell others that you do not have respect.

Past experience about the word: When a person's question is answered, either verbally or in writing; if we say it with anger the point will not be taken. When it is said in a professional manner it will be understood and if we say it with disrespect the point will not be taken.

Tips: Sometimes answering someone's questions can give a person the response they did not want to hear. It might be best, in some instances, to tell what circumstances you based your decision on, rather than answer the question first.

Date for applying your change?

What personally has to happen for a change to occur?

Two weeks after the change occurred; what changes happened at the workplace and in your personal life?

The only thing to do with good advice is to pass it on. It is never of any use oneself.—**Oscar Wilde**

Communication

Word: Communication
Word Definition: To express thoughts or messages

How you and others can benefit: Today, communicating is a loss art. Yesterday it used to be a way of life. People in today's time do not express to others what they feel or what they are going through, whether it is at the workplace or in their personal life. Sometimes you have to ask yourself if you really care, or want to understand what another person is saying or thinking.

Past experience about the word: I have found it best for myself to take the time to know my coworkers and others that are in personal life. I have found you are only given so many true friends. The more you communicate with others the more you will be cultivating those relationships, both at work and in your personal life.

Tips: Have you ever been around co-workers or family members that do not know how to communicate with each other? Without effectively communicating, this could lead to someone trying to second guess what the others are saying and doing. It has been said that if you tell someone something, then you tell it to them again, then you ask them to tell you what you told them, they should understand what is being said. I have seen in some cases this has to be done two to three times before the person understands what you are trying to get them to comprehend.

Date for applying your change?

What personally has to happen for a change to occur?

Two weeks after the change occurred; what changes happened at the workplace and in your personal life?

Making the simple complicated is commonplace; making the complicated simple, awesomely simple, that's creativity.
Charles Mingus

Passion

Word: Passion
Word Definition: Emotion or feeling

How you and others can benefit: Passion can be used in many different ways. It can be used at the workplace and at home. When someone has passion for the workplace it intrigues the mind of others. Sometimes when people have passion it is like they are being consumed by a roaring fire, and at times that passion can spread to others.

Past experience about the word: Passion can either turn someone for the circumstance or cause, and then they will either jump on that band-wagon or it may turn someone off. No matter passionate you are for something, it will not cause others to change their point of view. My suggestion is, go with your heart and listen to that inner voice of reason.

Tips: Do you have passion for your place of employment or in your personal life? If you watch your attitude you will know how much passion you have in those areas of your life. Your attitude will always show what lies on your heart and in most cases, your voice will indicate what is in your heart. If you do not want others to know your passion, learn to control your passion.

Date for applying your change?

What personally has to happen for a change to occur?

Two weeks after the change occurred; what changes happened at the workplace and in your personal life?

He who begins many things finishes but few.—**German Proverb**

Description

Word: Description:
Word Definition: A report of describing something

How you and others can benefit: When writing or describing something it should be kept as simple and as clear as possible. I would suggest that you make a rough draft of the subject you are describing and let another person read it. If that person understands what you are saying about that subject write the final description. If they do not understand, I would make the needed changes. Keep it in elementary terms so everyone will have a better understanding of the subject.

Past experience about the word: I found the fewer notes that are taken, the more you will forget about the subject you are trying to describe. The more notes that are taken in simple terms, the better you and others will understand the subject.

Tips: When describing a circumstance we need to put the description in the most elementary terms as we can. When this is completed, others including ourselves will understand what we are describing.

Date for applying your change?

What personally has to happen for a change to occur?

Two weeks after the change occurred; what changes happened at the workplace and in your personal life?

Think like a man of action, act like a man of thought.
—Henri Bergson

Emotion

Word: Emotion
Word Definition: A strong feeling; fear, sorrow, joy, hate, love are emotions

How you and others can benefit: Emotions at the workplace can work either leave on with a positive or a negative message. Emotions should be distinguished between being professional or personal. This is an area that needs to be under control. Never let your emotions get the best of you in a negative way because others can use it against you.

Past experience about the word: When you are working with a client and the client is in an emotional state, their emotions will hinder them from making a decision. What I would do is let the client know that it might be in their best interest for you to reschedule for another day and time. What I have done in the past is find all the needed information for that decision to be made and when I am meeting with the client for the second time, I review the circumstances that lead to the meeting. If they get emotional I would tell them how and what lead to the decision. I found out when you are upset about something it is best to look at the circumstances that lead to the problem. In some cases it will give you a better understanding about the decision. Remember, you can not reason with someone who is unreasonable.

Tips: Each chapter in LACK has a section on body language. It would be in your best interest to carefully read and understand the body language sections. Try this in your personal life and you will see others in a different light and how they respond to you. Then try this at the workplace; you will be able to understand what they are saying by their body language before they even say a word.

Date for applying your change?

What personally has to happen for change to occur?

Two weeks after the change occurred; what changes happened at the workplace and in your personal life?

Success is how high you bounce when you hit bottom.
—**General George S. Patton**

Distracted

Word: Distracted
Word Definition: To be diverted or side tracked

How you and others can benefit: How many times when you are trying to complete a project and you are distracted. What I have found is the best way to get your work completed and have a happy co-worker is to do the following: when they start up a conversation, suggest that you schedule a certain date and time for lunch and during lunch give them the time they need to talk.

Past experience about the word: I have found that once I am distracted, to get myself back on course, I will start saying to myself "if I do not complete this work at the office today, I will have to finish it at home," that will usually put me back on track.

Tips: If you do not distract others; others, in most cases, will not distract you.

Date for applying you're your change?

What personally has to happen for a change to occur?

Two weeks after the change occurred; what changes happened at the workplace and in your personal life?

The wise man never loses his temper.
Cicero

Gratitude

Word: Gratitude
Word Definition: Thankfulness

How you and others can benefit: We need to show gratitude to our clients for using our product and services. In today's business world the competition could be just a telephone call, a letter, or a meeting away from making your client their client. We can also show gratitude by giving our clients the best goods and service we can provide. We need to show our gratitude to our family and friends when they perform acts of kindness for us.

Past experience about the word: When we appreciate what others have done for us; our attitude toward others will be more giving than receiving.

Tips: Showing gratitude shows kindness to others and lets others know that their labor is well appreciated.

Date for applying your change?

What personally has to happen for change to occur?

Two weeks after the change occurred; what changes happened at the workplace and in your personal life?

The illiterate of the 21st century will not be those who cannot read and write, but those who cannot learn, unlearn, and relearn.
Alvin Toffler

Repeat

Word: Repeat
Word Definition: To say or do something over again

How you and others can benefit: By taking notes when you are on the telephone or meeting with a client it will leave a positive impression. Not paying attention and not taking notes will leave a negative impression. Asking them to repeat themselves over and over again will only send them to your competitor.

Past experience about the word: I have found that the more times I review my notes for a speech or seminar, the more my message will flow and be natural. The more natural you are in front of people, the more attentive they will be. Repeating yourself again and again will only lose the attention of the ones you are speaking to.

Tips: In business you should always try to find new techniques that work with clients. This can be the ice breaker for making the sale. In a different manner, one should never change their level standards from client to client as well as family member to family member. Others should always know your companies standards and knowledge about the product, this will lead to repeated business.

Date for applying your change?

What personally has to happen for change to occur?

Two weeks after the change occurred; what changes happened at the workplace and in your personal life?

In the long run, men only hit what they aim at.
—Henry David Thoreau

Anticipate

Word: Anticipate
Word Definition: To hope for, looking forward to

How you and others can benefit: When a person leaves for work, sometimes you wonder if that person makes the comment, "I am going to really make some major mistakes today." Our employer anticipates that we are not going to make mistakes when we use all the tools that are at our disposal. These tools could be programs, information needed by our associates or questions answered. We need to understand they are there to help us to succeed at our every day task, our obligation is to ask. Most of the time when we can complete our task correctly, someone else anticipates that our work being is completed correctly, due to there task is depends on our task being completed.

Past experience about the word: Everyone anticipates things in our life. When I hear that someone is foreseeing something to happen in there career, I will always tell them to weight the positive outcome and the negative outcome.

Tips: Anticipation can be positive or negative; the circumstance could go either way. When others know that we are anticipating something to happen in our career or personal life, they want to know the final outcome.

Date for applying your change?

What personally has to happen for change to occur?

Two weeks after the change occurred; what changes happened at the workplace and in your personal life?

Whenever you find you are on the side of the majority, it is time to pause and reflect.
Mark Twain [Samuel Langhornne Clemens] (1835-1910)

Awareness

Word: Awareness
Word Definition: Being mindful or being conscious

How you and others can benefit: When we are working with others we need to be aware of the employer's work ethics. Our speech and mannerisms need to be respectful to others and especially to clients and future clients. Treat others how you want to be treated.

Past experience about the word: Be aware that an unconscious decision we make can affect your relationship with your employer, co worker, friends and especially family members.

Tips: We need to be aware of how we treat others at the workplace or at home. When we are not aware of how we treat others, our level of respect for others is being lowered.

Date for applying your change?

What personally has to happen for change to occur?

Two weeks after the change occurred; what changes happened at the workplace and in your personal life?

History is the version of past events that people have decided to agree upon.
Napoleon Bonaparte

Body Language

Understanding body language can be an effective tool to help you understand clients, co-workers, friends, family members and your own feelings in situations. Monitoring your own body language can also help put others at ease.

Setting an Image:
Making eye contact
Nodding their head
Blinking at a fast rate

Being passionate:
Feet under chair
Standing on tip toes
Leaning forward

Observing:
Putting their leg on their knee
Stroking their chin with their hand
Looking up and right

Understanding body language can help you to interpret other people's mood, and learn how to work with a situation more effectively. This will help determine which approach to take in various circumstances.

Notes

<u>NOTES</u>

▼

CHAPTER 2

ACCOUNTABLE THE A OF LACK

Word: Accountable
Word Definition: Being responsible for ones actions

Have you ever tried to discuss with someone the accountability they have to others. If that person understands that they are accountable, they will show others they have a level of accountability. It will also indicate to others that they are responsible for their actions. I have seen in different situations that a lot of people will not accept accountability for their actions, whether it is something they said at the workplace or something in their personal life. We have to realize that we bare the responsibility for our actions and the consequences for our actions that are associated.

Not having accountability is paving the road to our personal destruction at the workplace, and at home. We need to set the same level of accountability of measurement for ourselves as we measure other people's level of accountability. It is our responsibility to keep and maintain a level of accountability in the workplace, and the standards that are set in our personal life. You will find that people will try to stay away from a person who does not accept accountability.

When you are not accountable to others you need to understand that you are indicating to others that you bare no responsibility for your actions with clients, friends, and family members and in time this will affect all your relationships.

The quality of accountability needs to be introduced at a young age. Parents need to teach their children that they are responsible for their actions. I can remember going to the toy store and I would see children throwing a temper tantrum on the floor. Then the parent would try to get the child to be quiet by telling them if they stop crying they can have a toy. The child is being rewarded for their actions. We have a responsibility to others by being accountable when someone is enraged about an issue when they are not being accountable for their actions. I remember when I managed a warranty department for a home builder and a home owner wanted to make a warranty claim. They proceeded to tell me that their garage wall needed to be repaired. I went to qualify the repair at the home, when I arrived they told me that their daughter drove their car through the garage wall. I told them that they need to call their insurance carrier and they told me that it is the builder's responsibility to repair the damage and it was not their daughter's fault. They did not want to be accountable for their actions and their daughter's actions. When a person is not accountable for their actions they want others to pay for their mistakes.

In this chapter the following pages have these corresponding topics under the main heading Accountability:
Understanding
Habit
Positive
Organizing
Commitment
Action
Dependable
Performance
Confidentially
Behavior
Preparation
Honest
Trustworthy
Factual
Reputation
Management
Body Language

Impossible things are simply those which so far have never been done.
—**Elbert Hubbard**

Habit

Word: Habit
Word Definition: A pattern of repetition, customary to ones daily manner or practice.

How you and others can benefit: A person can have a bad habit as well as a good habit. Before a bad habit can be broken the person must recognize that they need to correct that habit. I have seen bad habits stunt a person's growth in the company they were employed by. This could be why someone is in the same occupational position for years, and why they are missing all of the promotions.

Past experience about the word: When a person recognizes that they are a reflection of the workplace they will start to make changes. Changes could be one of the following: they need to increase their level of knowledge on computers, letter writing, contract negotiations, communication skills, how they work with clients and how they work with other associates.

Tips: When someone tells another person that their habit is stunting their growth, they should take time to examine themselves and make a change if needed.

Date for applying your change?

What personally has to happen for a change to occur?

Two weeks after the change occurred; what changes happened at the workplace and in your personal life?

Half the work that is done in this world is to make things appear what they are not.
Elias Root Beadle

Positive

Word: Positive
Word Definition: Having no doubt, being certain, being confident

How you and others can benefit: By having a positive attitude you will indicate to others that you are confident in what you are doing. You should understand that at your place of employment or in your personal life, if you are not positive on how to complete something or how something should be conducted or handled. Then you should ask for guidance in that area to gain confidence.

Past experience about the word: I can remember when I was working for a homebuilder and I found a problem with the structural points concerning a certain type of home being built. I went back to review the plans and found out that the framing contractor did not build the home according to the architectural blue prints. Before I took the problem to the president of the company, I went ahead and inspected other homes for this potential problem and found that the same problem was consistent in that type of home.

Tips: Do not confuse being positive with being arrogant. When a person is arrogant, in most cases they are selfish and only want personal gain.

Date for applying your change?

What personally has to happen for a change to occur?

Two weeks after the change occurred; what changes happened at the workplace and in your personal life?

"We must walk consciously only part way toward our goal, and then leap in the dark to our success."
—Henry David Thoreau

<u>Organizing</u>

Word: Organizing
Word Definition: To arrange, or to plan or coordinating

How you and others can benefit: Being organized will help you complete assignments and projects. Being organized is essential to your employer and it will help you build a working relationship with your coworkers and clients. Others will see you as an asset rather than a negative influence to the group. Organization can also benefit your personal life; others will want to know your organizing techniques.

Past experience about the word: People at your place of employment or in your personal life will see how being organized has helped you in your career. Others will ask you for guidance and being organized can save you time and money.

Tips: If you wanted to go on a vacation would you organize the day to day travel arrangements or would you just get in the car and drive? What would happen if you could not find any lodging while you were on vacation? When we plan accordingly we will see the results in a more positive manner. When we are not organized the responsibilities that need to be accomplished in that time frame will not be completed. If one has the trait of organization others will reap the benefit from your trait.

Date for applying your change?

What personally has to happen for a change to occur?

Two weeks after the change occurred; what changes happened at the workplace and in your personal life?

Our life is frittered away by detail. Simplicity, simplicity, simplicity! I say, let your affairs be as two or three, and not a hundred or a thousand; instead of a million, count half a dozen, and keep your accounts on your thumb-nail.
—**Henry D. Thoreau**

Commitment

Word: Commitment
Word Definition: pledging ones self to a position on some issue

How you and others can benefit: Knowing that an individual his committed should indicate to you that they will stay with that task or problem until it has been accomplished.

Past experience about the word: I can remember when I was working for a home builder and out of the five staff members I knew who was committed to complete their responsibilities and who was not. Those who were committed and completed their daily responsibilities were rewarded with salary increases. Those who were not committed and did not complete their responsibilities were eventually replaced by others who would.

Tips: Remember, when you make a promise or pledge your reputation you will be remembered by the out come of the commitment. If you complete your pledge or promise others will profess you are a person of your word. My advice would be, when making a commitment outline the dates, circumstances, specifics and completion date. Budget your time wisely until the task or project is completed.

Date for applying your change?

What personally has to happen for a change to occur?

Two weeks after the change occurred; what changes happened at the workplace and in your personal life?

Always bear in mind that your own resolution to succeed is more important than any one thing.
—**Abraham Lincoln**

Action

Word: Action
Word Definition: A person's behavior or conduct

How you and others can benefit: When a person's actions are in a professional manner you will know that their behavior or conduct indicates that they have high standards.

Past experience about the word: Remember the old saying "an action speaks louder than words?" People will always judge a person by two things: their actions and their words.

Tips: How many times are we caught doing something we should not be doing? How we respond to others is how others will respond to us. In some cases, that could be happiness with happiness or it could be rudeness with rudeness. The action is in us not others, so do not confuse who's to blame.

Date for applying your change?

What personally has to happen for a change to occur?

Two weeks after the change occurred; what changes happened at the workplace and in your personal life?

Happy the man, and happy he alone,
Who can all today his own;
He who, secure within, can say,
Tomorrow do thy worst, for I have lived today.
—John Dryden

Dependable

Word: Dependable
Word Definition: Reliable, trustworthy

How you and others can benefit: Knowing someone is dependable will indicate to others that they can meet their daily obligations. They understand what time management is.

Past experience about the word: I have found that when you work with others you will know who is going to be dependable and who will be. Those who do not have this trait will go through life watching others who are dependable get promoted and move ahead in the business world. When someone notices that they need to have this trait they will understand why they missed out on before. It is better to make that change now and look ahead rather than look back.

Tips: Being dependable means understanding time management; knowing when it is time to move onto the next obligation. One trait of a dependable person is to write down the next day's obligations, time frames, and some information about the obligations that will give you a reference point to becoming dependable.

Date for applying your change?

What personally has to happen for a change to occur?

Two weeks after the change occurred; what changes happened at the workplace and in your personal life?

Life is made up, not of great sacrifices or duties, but of little things, in which smiles and kindness, and small obligations, given habitually, are what win and preserve the heart, and secure comfort.
—Sir H. Davy

Performance

Word: Performance
Word Definition: one who gives a presentation before an audience

How you and others can benefit: For someone's performance to be outstanding it takes time and dedication. When time and dedication are put into ones everyday practice, whether it is at work or home, you will see positive results. You will also reap the benefits.

Past experience about the word: I have found the more time I prepare for a meeting by obtaining all the required material and information, the more successful the meeting will be. When one spends not enough time and gathers very little information their performance could be a disaster.

Tips: Every day there are people in our workplace or personal life that are watching our every day actions. We have to understand that our actions do reflect others and those actions can build someone's confidence in us or destroy it.

Date for applying your change?

What personally has to happen for a change to occur?

Two weeks after the change occurred; what changes happened at the workplace and in your personal life?

Do not look where you fell, but where you slipped.
—**African Proverb**

Confidentially

Word: Confidentially
Word Definition: One who has been trusted with private information

How you and others can benefit: Confidentially is something that a person has to be cautious about; that is sharing personal information. It takes time to build trust in a relationship whether at work or in your personal life. Some individuals will share confidential information for their personal gain. One needs to understand that it is in their best interest to keep all information private unless you want it to be public knowledge.

Past experience about the word: I have seen business partnerships dissolve, friendships lost and family members disowned when someone betrays ones trust by not keeping information private or confidential.

Tips: I have found that when you are asked to keep things confidential and someone is asked about what you have been told, it needs to be kept confidential. When someone asks, I will tell them that I cannot comment on that question. If they ask again then I tell them if they bring up the question again I will have to leave.

Date for applying your change?

What personally has to happen for a change to occur?

Two weeks after the change occurred; what changes happened at the workplace and in your personal life?

There is no success without hardship.
—**Sophocles**

Behavior

Word: Behavior
Word Definition: A person's demeanor, action, reaction, acting under certain circumstances

How you and others can benefit: Whether you're reading the newspaper or watching the news you will find out daily about the private lives of movie stars and athletes. I remember hearing about what was going to happen to one of the top quarterbacks in the NFL for his part in a dog fighting operation. Because of his inappropriate behavior he has lost his career and may end up with jail time due to his behavior. We have to understand that our behavior will show others whether we have a good or bad reputation.

Past experience about the word: How we act just does not affect us but also affects others. We have to understand that we are responsible for our actions and the outcome of our behavior. Also, others will judge us for our actions.

Tips: Our daily actions will show others our behavior. We have to constantly keep our behavior in check so circumstances will not lead to personal destruction.

Date for applying your change?

What personally has to happen for a change to occur?

Two weeks after the change occurred; what changes happened at the workplace and in your personal life?

Keep steadily before you the fact that all true success depends at last upon yourself.
—Theodore T. Munger

Preparation

Word: Preparation
Word Definition: One who is making a provision, the process of preparing

How you and others can benefit: Taking the time to prepare for a project or task needs to be a habit. Without preparing, results can be disastrous at your place of employment and in your personal life. This is a trait that everyone should strive for; it takes 21 days for a habit to your daily obligation. When one has this trait others will see the benefits of this trait, for example would you give a speech without preparation? Would you retire today, when you have not saved anything?

Past experience about the word: When someone is prepared it can lead to employment advancements. Your coworkers would rather work with a person that comes prepared than with a person who is always unprepared. Those in your personal life will benefit from this trait.

Tips: It is best to take time to plan and prepare for a project it is to begin the project with out counting the cost, time and money. Preparing will get you closer to completion, not being prepared will lead to loss of time that can never be accounted for. Once that time is gone you can not get it back. Prepare wisely!

Date for applying your change?

What personally has to happen for change to occur?

Two weeks after the change occurred; what changes happened at the workplace and in your personal life?

Write down the advice of him who loves you, though you like it not at present.
—English Proverb

Honest

Word: Honest
Word Definition: Truthfulness, having integrity and being upright

How you and others can benefit: It is better to be honest than to be deceitful. Demonstrating honesty will indicate to others that you are a person of your word. Sowing deceitfulness will indicate others that you can not be trusted.

Past experience about the word: I have found that people would rather hear the truth than hear a sugar coated lie.

Tips: It is best to tell it like it is rather than to decorate a lie because the decorated lie will always lead to distrust and shame. Someone who is dishonest will never have a reputable reputation unless they change.

Date for applying your change?

What personally has to happen for change to occur?

Two weeks after the change occurred; what changes happened at the workplace and in your personal life?

"Try not to become a man of success but rather try to become a man of value."
—Albert Einstein

Trustworthy

Word: Trustworthy
Word Definition: one who deserves trust, being dependable

How you and others can benefit: You can determine by someone's speech and actions whether they are trustworthy. When you know someone that has this trait, in most cases you shouldn't have to worry about that person betraying your trust. When one is trusted they also understand that they are accountable to others for their actions.

Past experience about the word: I have found when one possesses this trait, in most cases they the following traits; accountability, loyalty, integrity.

Tips: When you are being trusted with company documents or being trusted by someone in your personal life not to share information, you need to understand that what you are being trusted with cannot be shared with coworkers, family or friends. Many times we damage or destroy our reputation by sharing the trusted information and betraying someone's trust.

Date for applying your change?

What personally has to happen for change to occur?

Two weeks after the change occurred; what changes happened at the workplace and in your personal life?

Let everyone ascertain his special business and calling, and then stick with it if he wants to be successful.
—**Benjamin Franklin**

Factual

Word: Factual
Word Definition: One who contains facts

How you and others can benefit: Understanding before a decision is made you need to have all the facts or information, that way the decision can be based on facts and information and not on hearsay.

Past experience about the word: Sometimes what is said about a person can be distorted, so the person makes the conversation more entertaining to ones attention. The advice I would give would be to understand that some individuals like to plant false seeds or spread false gossip about coworkers, friends or family. The question I would ask myself what rumors are they spreading around about me? I would suggest that one should ask for the facts in writing before a decision is made. This should indicate to you to keep records and information up to date and always add new information when new information is obtained.

Tips: Understand that our words can build up individuals as well as tear them down individuals. When we are being asked to take part in gossip or slander we need to walk away. The only time we should take part in that type of conversation is when we are being asked by our superiors at the place of employment or by law.

Date for applying your change?

What personally has to happen for a change to occur?

Two weeks after the change occurred; what changes happened at the workplace and in your personal life?

The only fool bigger than the person who knows it all is the person who argues with him.
Stanislaw Jerszy Lec (1909-)

Reputation

Word: Reputation
Word Definition: Peoples opinion of a person's character

How you and others can benefit: Remember, a person's reputation can influence others at the workplace or at home. Most people would rather be associated with a person who has a good name. Who you are associated with will determine other people's attitude and opinion about you.

Past experience about the word: Something I told a friend of mine about a person's reputation "your name you are given at birth; how you live your life determines peoples opinion about a person, when you die your name and reputation are all that people will remember you by."

Tips: You should have the same reputation at the workplace as you do in your personal life. When they are not the same you should ask yourself what areas you need to change. Life is about changes and a person that can change for the good can make the difference, not just in themselves but also in others.

Date for applying your change?

What personally has to happen for change to occur?

Two weeks after the change occurred; what changes happened at the workplace and in your personal life?

The better part of happiness is to wish to be what you are.
—Desiderius Erasmus

Management

Word: Management
Word Definition: One who supervises or directs employees at the workplace

How you and others can benefit: Management should know the performance standards of the product and services that they are providing to clients. They also need to understand how to manage their employees or associates and be accountable for their actions to their employer. A manager has to understand that when one of their associates does not understand the concept that they are trying to teach, they need to try various approaches to help their associate understand. I found that the more training you have the easier it is to change the text or the method on that subject you are training. It is management's responsibility to give an associate all the training they need so they can succeed at their place of employment. It is the responsibility of the employee to retain that information and use it for the client; and to better the business they represent.

Past experience about the word: It is the teacher's responsibility to adapt the lesson or the subject to the student(s). The method you use with one might not work with others; you need to be adaptable.

Tips: Management should be considered like a college course, sometimes it could be called the College Course of Hard Knocks and sometimes the College of Learning; it should never be called the College of Failure. What works for some companies may not work for other companies. Management is like a journey, at the end of the journey our clients and employees will understand our product and services.

Date for applying your change?

What personally has to happen for change to occur?

Two weeks after the change occurred; what changes happened at the workplace and in your personal life?

Dreams and dedication are a powerful combination.
—**William Longgood**

Body Language

Understanding body language can be an effective tool to help you understand clients, co-workers, friends, family members and your own feelings in situations. Monitoring your own body language can also help put others at ease.

Being alert:
Standing
Arms behind back
Smile

Being positive:
Chin up
Leaning forward

Understanding body language can help you to interpret clients, co-workers, friends and family member's mood, and how to work with a situation more effectively. This will determine which approach to take in various circumstances.

NOTES

<u>Notes</u>

▼

CHAPTER 3

CREDIBLE THE C OF LACK

Word: Credible
Word Definition: One who is believable, trustworthy, and reliable

When a person looks at a person's reputation they look at ones good credibility along with the qualities that are not so good. It has been said that when a person meets another person for the first time, the first seven seconds will indicate to a person about someone's credibility. Then they will make a decision with the facts and circumstances about that person's credibility.

Everyone has areas in their life that need work. The first thing you have to be is honest with ourselves on what those areas are, that way we can start to make those life long changes so our credibility can benefit us and others. When a person understands that there are areas in their life that need to be changed they need to look at how they can benefit from that change. They will be credible in the eyes of others. Friends and co-workers will want to be involved with you at the workplace and in your personal life. Your career can benefit from the change, employers and others will see a more potential in your career. Clients will be more willing to work with you and they will have more trust in what you are saying.

It has been said that all you will leave this world only with your name. People will always remember the good things or the bad things that a person has done in their life. So if you say you are trustworthy do not wave from the truth, if you want others to believe what you have said, do not add or take away from the truth. If you want to reliable never break a promise.

On the personal side, we have to understand that who we associate with will influence us and others will judge our credibility. Our credibility can help your employer choose between you and someone else when there is a promotion opportunity at your place of employment. People will believe what you are saying instead of not believing what you have said. People will judge a person by their reputation more than what accomplishments that a person has had in their life.

In this chapter the following pages have these corresponding topics under the main heading Credible:
Believable
Documentation
Vision
Empathy
Concern
Responsible
Attitude
Loyalty
Enthusiastic
Circumstances
Body Language

The ability to convert ideas to things is the secret of outward success.
—Henry Ward Beecher

Believable

Word: Believable
Word Definition: Being truthful or real

How you and others can benefit: When you are at work or at home how do others see you? How true are you to those around you? Do you add little bit to what is being said to make the story more adventurous? When others at the workplace or in your personal life catch you not being someone they can trust and believe; they will, in most cases, disregard what you have said in the past.

Past experience about the word: When a person tells the truth at all times, whether I like the answer or not, then that person is believable. If a person sways from the truth they are called a liar. I will send my business to the person who I can trust.

Tips: When you start telling others something that is not believable others will not trust what you have been saying and doing in the past. Being truthful at all times and there will be no question that you're believable. For example, if somebody asks you to comment on their hairstyle, use as few words as possible.

Date for applying your change?

What personally has to happen for a change to occur?

Two weeks after the change occurred; what changes happened at the workplace and in your personal life?

Do just once what others say you can't do, and you will never pay attention to their limitations again?
James R. Cook

Documentation

Word: Documentation
Word Definition: Keeping written record

How you and others can benefit: Have you ever heard the saying "a picture is worth a thousand words." The same is true about documentation. What would happen if you are meeting with a client and they are telling you their thoughts and information about the product(s) you are trying to get them to buy; as you are repeating the conversation to your supervisor you cannot remember some of the explicit details about their concern on the product. Wouldn't that be an embarrassing moment? What if you were sent to the store for some items that were needed for a dinner party and you forgot some of the needed items. That would lead to a discussion with the person that sent you to the store, before the guests arrived.

Past experience about the word: It has been said that a person can only comprehend 10% of the information that they are given. If that is true with most people, then documentation would give that person a better handle in there personal life and their career. I have found that it best to carry a small memo book in my pocket for memory notes, and for a list. A PDA also will be very useful in this area

Tips: When meeting with a client or a potential client it is best to outline the topics that are being discussed on paper or on a PDA; this will give you a reference point to refer back to this meeting when needed.

Date for applying your change?

What personally has to happen for a change to occur?

Two weeks after the change occurred; what changes happened at the workplace and in your personal life?

This report, by its very length, defends itself against the risk of being read.
Winston Churchill (1874-1965)

<u>Vision</u>

Word: Vision
Word Definition: Having foresight

How you and others can benefit: Some people have enough vision to see the success of a company in the near future. It could even be the attitude of seeing things positively in different areas of ones career and personal life. What if a person wanted the changes to be made in a certain time frame, which included making some dramatic changes in ones life? They noticed the need and it came about because they had a vision, and they could see that they would have a more productive life after they made a change. Then that change took place, that person could say they had a vision on how things could be after the needed change.

Past experience about the word: When one has a vision for their career and personal life, they need understand that sometimes what follows a vision is fear. Fear will give you reasons why you should not trust your vision. But when that vision can better yourself and others, you need go on faith and a person should think things through when making any change in a career or personal life.

Tips: We need to try to see all aspects in every situation and when we blind ourselves from seeing it other ways we are limiting our potential and vision.

Date for applying your change?

What personally has to happen for a change to occur?

Two weeks after the change occurred; what changes happened at the workplace and in your personal life?

Never express yourself more clearly than you are able to think.
Niels Bohr (1885-1962)

<u>Empathy</u>

Word: Empathy
Word Definition: Identify with ones feelings or motive

How you and others can benefit: You need to understand that working with others at the workplace or in their personal life, there will be times when ones emotions can get the best of any person. This is when you need to apply the Golden Rule: Treat Others as You Want to be Treated. When this is followed all will benefit and have a better understanding what a friend or caring person really is.

Past experience about the word: Sometimes I had to be, what I will call, the whipping post for others emotions and feelings; especially when you have some clients that are not happy with your product or service. After they blow their needed steam, I usually tell them I understand the situation but I am not here to be verbally abused. I am here to correct the situation if needs to be corrected and if the situation is correct, I am here to restate the standards of the product.

Tips: This is a time when a true opinion or feeling will be seen by others, and in a relationship it will be where others will really know where you are in life. Some say it is weak to weep, others say it is strong to weep and want to know what the heart bares.

Date for applying your change?

What personally has to happen for a change to occur?

Two weeks after the change occurred; what changes happened at the workplace and in your personal life?

The man who never makes a mistake always takes orders from one who does.

No man or woman who tries to pursue an ideal in his or her own way is without enemies.
Daisy Bates (1863-1951)

Concern

Word: Concern
Word Definition: Having interest or relating to

How you and others can benefit: How many times have you been around someone that is not bothered by anything? Maybe it is a time frame on a project, whether it is in their personal life or their career. I would have to say that being concerned can be a good trait and a person becoming over concerned could border on being compulsive. What would determine if a person was being concerned or if they were being compulsive would be their attitude. That is why a person has to have balance. When they do not have balance, areas of their life will be affected.

Past experience about the word: I get concerned when I delegate responsibilities to others and they show very little concern or enthusiasm about the project. Sometimes, after the responsibility has been accomplished by others, I will recognize that I wasted a great part of my time and energy worrying about that project when I could have been spent more time being productive in other areas of my life.

Tips: When we are interested in what others are going through whether it is in their personal life or in their career, at times that concern needs to be backed up by action. That could be by making a telephone call, e-mail, or a letter. In life you are given neighbors and co-workers, but how many can you say you have kindred friendships with. Being concerned at times does mean being involved.

Date for applying your change?

What personally has to happen for a change to occur?

Two weeks after the change occurred; what changes happened at the workplace and in your personal life?

Consult: to seek another's advice on a course already decided upon.
—**Ambrose Pierce**

Responsible

Word: Responsible
Word Definition: Being accountable for something

How you and others can benefit: By understanding that we are liable for our actions. When you are working on a project with someone who gives you the impression that they are not responsible for their actions that project becomes difficult. What needs to be accomplished is for that person to be made aware by their supervisor that everyone is responsible for their actions. A scheduled meeting with the supervisor and all the employees who are working on that project will ensure everyone in that meeting will have a better understanding on what is expected. After that meeting, when they are still not being responsible for their part in the project, I would inform the supervisor so they will understand when others have to pick up the slack. Most of today's work force needs to understand the meaning of responsibility, there are still are a few that believe they are an exception to the rules of the workplace and life

Past experience about the word: One weekend two of my friends borrowed some of my tools. They both told me that they would only need the tools for that weekend. The one friend brought the tool back the next day. The other friend said he wasn't finished with it, and next weekend he would bring the tool back. It has been over two years and he still has not returned the tools.

Tips: Remember, being responsible is also about being accountable for actions and at times the actions of others who we are responsible for, either at work or home.

Date for applying your change?

What personally has to happen for a change to occur?

Two weeks after the change occurred; what changes happened at the workplace and in your personal life?

As a general rule, the most successful man in life is the man who has the best information.
—**Benjamin Disraeli**

Attitude

Word: Attitude
Word Definition: The feeling one has for oneself, others and situations

How you and others can benefit: Your attitude will help you climb the ladder of success in you career. Your attitude will make or break you in today's society. Our attitude at home will either strengthen a relationship with family members or it will deteriorate them. One who has a good attitude will always be willing to do what it takes to get the task accomplished. Especially when there are difficult circumstances, a positive attitude will help others have a positive outlook.

Past experience about the word: I work with a couple of different businesses and one of those businesses there was an individual that had a very negative attitude, and his attitude started to affect the attitude of others. I talked to that individual about them having a more positive outlook on business and life. One of the ways that I did this was by asking him whether he saw the glass as hall full or half empty. He stated the glass was half empty and I told him the positive outlook was to look at the glass half full. It took two weeks of working with him for his perspective to change.

Tips: A person with a good attitude will always be remembered as a team player. A good attitude is ready to face what tomorrow brings. A person with a bad attitude will never be happy when the circumstances in life get challenging.

Date for applying your change?

What personally has to happen for a change to occur?

Two weeks after the change occurred; what changes happened at the workplace and in your personal life?

To win without risk is to triumph without glory.
—Corneille

<u>Loyalty</u>

Word: Loyalty
Word Definition: Having allegiance

How you and others can benefit: When you have someone who is in your center of influence a coworker or friend that has the trait of being loyal, you need to realize how fortunate you are. In today's society it is a gift because some individuals will betray others for personal gain.

Past experience about the word: I have seen when a person has this quality in their life they usually will start climbing the ladder to success, either in the business world or in their personal life.

Tips: Being loyal is not defined as showing betrayal. By being loyal one should understand that whatever the circumstances are, you will not be disloyal by conduct or betray any knowledge about business or personal matters. It also means that your allegiance will never waiver and last forever.

Date for applying your change?

What personally has to happen for change to occur?

Two weeks after the change occurred; what changes happened at the workplace and in your personal life?

Fear the goat from the front, the horse from the rear, and the man from all sides.
—Russian Proverb

Enthusiastic

Word: Enthusiastic
Word Definition: Having excitement

How you and others can benefit: The more someone is excited about their career or personal life the more that enthusiasm you will spark in others.

Past experience about the word: The more you are enthusiastic about your product and services, clients and customers will share that enthusiasm, which will spark the interest in others.

Tips: It is a proven factor, if a person is excited about their home life and workplace, which enthusiasm will help them and others meet their potential.

Date for applying your change?

What personally has to happen for change to occur?

Two weeks after the change occurred; what changes happened at the workplace and in your personal life?

Making the simple complicated is commonplace; making the complicated simple, awesomely simple, that's creativity.
Charles Mingus

Circumstance

Word: Circumstance
Word Definition: Knowing the facts about a condition before a decision is being made.

How you and others can benefit: When making a decision, all conditions and anything pertaining to that circumstance needs to be considered.

Past experience about the word: When I have to make a decision I will gather all the information regarding that circumstance. Then, I will review all the information and circumstances before I make my decision.

Tips: When making a decision all circumstances that lead to a major decision need to be considered. An honest decision can then be made on how to achieve closure on that circumstance. The decision cannot be based on the personal gain of the one who is making that final decision. The decision has to be entirely based on all of the circumstances and information.

Date for applying your change?

What personally has to happen for change to occur?

Two weeks after the change occurred; what changes happened at the workplace and in your personal life?

All truly wise thoughts have been thought already thousands of times; but to make them truly ours, we must think them over again honestly, till they take root in our personal experience.
Johann Wolfgang von Goethe (1749-1832)

Body Language

Understanding body language can be an effective tool to help you understand clients, co-workers, friends, family members and your own feelings in situations. Monitoring your own body language can also help put others at ease.

Being belligerent:
Leaning their body forward
Shaking their fist
Pointing their finger at you

Being defensive:
Standing stiff
Clenching their hands
Turning their head so they cannot hear what you are saying

Understanding body language can help you to interpret the clients, co-workers, friends and family member's mood, and how to work with a situation more effectively. This will help determine on what approach to take in that circumstance.

NOTES

NOTES

CHAPTER 4

▼

KNOWLEDGE THE K OF
LACK

Word: Knowledge
**Word Definition: Having awareness or an understanding gained
through experience**

It is our responsibility to have knowledge about the products or services the
company we are employed by offers. This can enhance our relationship with our
clients and advance our career. We have to understand that knowledge is power
and not having knowledge will deprive our clients, as well as our employer, and
will hinder our career advancement. Also, not having knowledge can cause one to
experience failure. Before a decision is made it is best to collect all the needed
information about that subject so circumstances.

Knowledge can be one of the greatest achievements a person can have;
understanding that the experiences in life can increase ones knowledge.
Knowledge should be shared so all can understand and grow from life problems
and blessings. The outcome of life's problems will hopefully keep us from making
the same daily mistakes. Knowledge is like a ladder leading you to places that
only the ones using and containing that knowledge will understand. Knowledge
should be shared.

On a personal note, having knowledge is a good thing but spouting off
knowledge every time you come in contact with someone can leave a negative

impression. My recommendation is to use your knowledge wisely. Share knowledge only when others will use it wisely and not to the ones who will use it selfishly.

In this chapter the following pages have these corresponding topics under the main heading Knowledge:
Reliable
Confident
Accuracy
Follow Through
Closure
Situation
Time
Quality
Expectation
Process
Pride
Succeed
Technique
Efficient
Focused
Stability
Body Language

Always bear in mind that your own resolution to succeed is more important than any one thing.
—**Abraham Lincoln**

Reliable

Word: Reliable
Word Definition: Dependable

How you and others can benefit: Having someone say you are reliable is a reputable trait. When someone knows you are reliable, others will want to work with you on projects or tasks. It also indicates that you are willing to complete the project or task when it takes time and determination to finish. Employers look for this trait in future managers.

Past experience about the word: I have found that when someone makes the remark that someone is reliable, for the most part you do not have to worry about that person being not dependable in this part of their work ethics.

Tips: I have found that the word reliable describes a lot of great attributes about co-workers, family members and others in your personal life. When someone you work with has this attribute give them a compliment and express that how much you enjoy working with someone that goes the extra mile.

Date for applying your change?

What personally has to happen for a change to occur?

Two weeks after the change occurred; what changes happened at the workplace and in your personal life?

The whole secret of a successful life is to find out what is one's destiny to do, and then do it.
—Henry Ford

<u>Confident</u>

Word: Confident
Word Definition: Self assurance

How you and others can benefit: This is a positive trait that can be a negative trait. On the positive side, someone with this trait can be used to build up others that lack confidence in him or herself and help others in difficult times at work or in their personal life. The negative side is sometimes being over confident leads to bragging.

Past experience about the word: I have seen when someone is confident about a decision that was made at the workplace or in ones personal life, the outcome of the decision turned out as they thought it would. When others see that person's confidence about that decision and that decision turns out to be a good investment. Whether it is money, time, project, task, relationship, etc., if that person is not boastful about their confidence, usually others will recognize this attribute and this can affect ones career in a positive manner.

Tips: Do not confuse being confident with being arrogant. Being confident is being assured about a circumstance or a situation. Being arrogant is only used for selfish gain.

Date for applying your change?

What personally has to happen for a change to occur?

Two weeks after the change occurred; what changes happened at the workplace and in your personal life?

Knowledge of what is possible is the beginning of happiness.
—**George Santayana**

Accuracy

Word: Accuracy
Word Definition: The fact of being accurate and not having mistakes

How you and others can benefit: Whether you are doing a task at home or work, when someone strives to complete a task without mistakes, you will find out that in most cases their will not be any lost time due to correcting errors. This can be done by taking your time and checking your work, so others will not find your mistakes.

Past experience about the word: I have found that when you start a project, time should be taken to check that project when it has been completed. It takes less time to correct the mistakes before others see the defect. Also, you will not face the embarrassment if your work is not accurate.

Tips: If we can manage our time at our place of employment and in our personal life, we will not have to spend too much time correcting mistakes on projects or tasks that should have been completed correctly in the first place. We need to plan our priorities before our priorities have no further plans with us.

Date for applying your change?

What personally has to happen for a change to occur?

Two weeks after the change occurred; what changes happened at the workplace and in your personal life?

The chief factor in any man's success or failure must be his own character.
—Theodore Roosevelt

Follow Through

Word: Follow Through
Word Definition: One who completes a process or finishes a task

How you and others can benefit: Having someone complete their daily task from start to finish will allow others time to complete their daily tasks and assignments. Doing this they will understand that they are responsible for completing their tasks and projects. When someone does not follow through on their daily task, not following through can affect others work, when their task depends on your task being completed. Someone not having this attribute can cost someone a promotion, job, and relationships. Someone who has this attribute can be appreciated by employment promotions, having better relationships with coworkers, better relationships with the ones in your personal life.

Past experience about the word: Follow through can be completed by following up with letters, voicemail, telephone or email. When following through is completed in a timely manner the outcome will be customer satisfaction.

Tips: When one masters the art of follow through they will realize that closure can be obtained in a timelier manner and the goal of customer satisfaction will be met.

Date for applying your change?

What personally has to happen for change to occur?

Two weeks after the change occurred; what changes happened at the workplace and in your personal life?

The ability to convert ideas to things is the secret of outward success.
—Henry Ward Beecher

Closure

Word: Closure
Word Definition: End or conclusion

How you and others can benefit: Closure is the final point that some individuals never achieve. When working with a client you have to achieve closure. If there is a disagreement with a client there has to be a final decision made so there will not be a misunderstanding about the decision. If you do not obtain closure there will be a problem or a circumstance without an ending. When closure is obtained all parties need to understand that nothing more will be done on that issue.

Past experience about the word: Closure, in my definition, should also indicate to a person that they understand what the provisions, product, services, and when the product will be received. This should indicate to them that once the product is received or services rendered, that the business agreement has been completed. When a decision has been made on a particular subject to achieve closure, I would follow-up all decisions with a letter covering that conversation and what lead to the decision. I also would carbon copy anyone that pertains to that circumstance or the decision which was made.

Tips: This can be one of the most difficult areas to achieve at the workplace or in the home. If closure is not achieved there will be no ending to the problem or condition.

Date for applying your change?

What personally has to happen for change to occur?

Two weeks after the change occurred; what changes happened at the workplace and in your personal life?

Success seems to be largely a matter of hanging on after others have let go.
—**William Feather**

Situation

Word: Situation
Word Definition: Ones position or circumstance

How you and others can benefit: Have you ever heard someone say, do not let your home life carry into the workplace? In today's working world their will be times that situations will arise and you will miss time from work. This could be due to a death, sickness, children etc. My suggestion to you is be completely honest. If you need to take time from work ask if you can work from home, until the situation gets resolved. Also, ask your employer for their opinion on what they would do if they were in your position.

Past experience about the word: We all have problems and sometimes our problems will cause us to miss work. One of the best qualities one could have would be honesty, be honest. I have found that when individuals are honest about their problems their employers are more willing to work with them through their problems.

Tips: When I have to miss work due to life's situations, I would ask my employer if I could work nights or weekends to make up my lost time.

Date for applying your change?

What personally has to happen for change to occur?

Two weeks after the change occurred; what changes happened at the workplace and in your personal life?

"Success is the necessary misfortune of life, but it is only to the very unfortunate that it comes early."
—Anthony Troloppe

<u>Time</u>

Word: Time
Word Definition: A number, as of years, days, minutes

How you and others can benefit: When a person can manage their time, in most cases they will respect other peoples time. A person that understands when time is being wasted, that lost time can never be regained. It will also cost other peoples time that are involved with you on projects, tasks or in your personal life.

Past experience about the word: When we are at the workplace and we need to give our employers a days work for a days pay, which we agreed to work for. We should not waste time with others, or waste time on the internet for personal use during work hours. When someone wastes time it could cause others to pay for that loss time, by having to stay late at work to complete that days task.

Tips: Time is an element that cannot be given back to a person once it is used, it should be spent wisely. If you do not count the cost of time at work and at home, others will not count the cost of time for you, then they are wasting your time and theirs.

Date for applying your change?

What personally has to happen for change to occur?

Two weeks after the change occurred; what changes happened at the workplace and in your personal life?

A smooth sea never made a skillful mariner.
—English Proverb

<u>Quality</u>

Word: Quality
Word Definition: Ones character, attitude

How you and others can benefit: Someone could have good qualities or a person could have some not so good qualities. At your place of employment one should give their employer 100 percent of quality time so their daily task or assignments can be completed. One has to determine to whose standards they are rating a person's qualities. Those day to day standards should be listed in an employee manual. Remember the quality of your work is a reflection on your reputation.

Past experience about the word: Quality and quantity do not have the same definition. Some people try to associate these words with the same definition. I have seen first hand when you try to have quality and quantity, the quality is what suffers.

Tips: A person needs to dedicate enough time so quality will be seen in their projects and daily task at the workplace, home and in their personal life. When conducting business at the workplace and when you are spending time with others at home do not confuse quality with quantity.

Date for applying your change?

What personally has to happen for change to occur?

Two weeks after the change occurred; what changes happened at the workplace and in your personal life?

I will not condemn you for what you did yesterday, if you do it right today.
Sheldon S. Maye

Expectation

Word: Expectation
Word Definition: An act or condition that has been set

How you and others can benefit: When you are setting an expectation, set an expectation that can be met. When setting an expectation one should consider all the steps that it will take to meet that expectation. When you set an expectation remember it is best to under-promise and over-deliver.

Past experience about the word: When you give someone what is expected per the contract or conversation you are meeting, in some cases you will be exceeding the expectation.

Tips: If you expect good things at the workplace you will reap good things. If you expect good things at home you will reap good things at home. It is better to expect in a positive manner than to have no expectation at all.

Date for applying your change?

What personally has to happen for change to occur?

Two weeks after the change occurred; what changes happened at the workplace and in your personal life?

To be absolutely certain about something, one must know everything or nothing about it.
Olin Miller

Process

Word: Process
Word Definition: The course or steps that lead to the ending result

How you and others can benefit: During the 1990's, procedure was the term that was developed and used for management. In the year 2000, the word procedure was changed to "process," which still has the same definition in the business world. When someone is working for a company they need to educate their employees on what the process is for that business. By having all the required information for an employee, employees will have a better understanding of what is expected at the workplace. After the employee has read and understands what is required, it can help eliminate any future problems. There needs to be classes on educating the employees on business ethics and performance at the workplace.

Past experience about the word: When a process is in place all have to adhere to the process for it to work. It will only work when it is enforced from the owner of the company down to the managers, supervisors and then to the associates. It has been a proven factor if an exception is made for one person in the process; eventually there will exceptions for all.

Tips: If we do not write down the steps it takes to complete a project at work or home how can our time and effort benefit others by our time and energy that was spent to complete that project. If we had someone to help us save time, our time could be spent helping others at the workplace or home.

Date for applying your change?

What personally has to happen for change to occur?

Two weeks after the change occurred; what changes happened at the workplace and in your personal life?

The further one goes, the less one knows."
Lao-tzu (sixth century BC), Legendary Chinese philosopher

Pride

Word: Pride

Word Definition: Proper or being justified and having self respect

How you and others can benefit: When someone loses pride they also lose self respect in most cases. We need to have pride in the workplace and at home. If you do not have pride and you are employed, you need to start showing pride by being thankful that you have a job and you are getting a paycheck. Also, by having pride that your employer hired you to do a job. Be prideful about your family. There are some people that do not have family or friends so start looking at the good side of things instead of the bad.

Past experience about the word: If more people would see the good in their job rather than the bad, their attitude would be positive and it could help instill pride in others. When individuals have pride in their work and in the product they produce, quality of the product and customer satisfaction will increase.

Tips: One should have pride for their employer and for the people in their life. Pride can lead to self destruction when a person exalts themselves more than others. This could lead to a down fall. It is necessary to have justified pride and not conceited pride.

Date for applying your change?

What personally has to happen for change to occur?

Two weeks after the change occurred; what changes happened at the workplace and in your personal life?

If you can't describe what you are doing as a process, you don't know what you're doing. W. Edwards Deming

Succeed

Word: Succeed
Word Definition: To complete something attempted

How you and others can benefit: A positive attitude will help you succeed in accomplishing a task or project that has been difficult. A negative attitude can cause a task or project to not be completed, which could lead to employees getting dismissed from their workplace. Success in life, projects, occupation, family and marriage is determined on a person's attitude. At a school near my home there is banner that is hung on the front of the school, which reads, "Your attitude determines your altitude." That is so true in today's attitude for a person to succeed.

Past experience about the word: I was told when someone succeeds at something it would help others if they would write down what it took for them to succeed, that way others may also share in their success.

Tips: Succeeding is a gift of accomplishment. Remember to write down which areas were more difficult than others. This accomplished knowledge can be shared with others so they can learn by your success.

Date for applying your change?

What personally has to happen for change to occur?

Two weeks after the change occurred; what changes happened at the workplace and in your personal life?

Do the right thing. It will gratify some people and astonish the rest.
Mark Twain [Samuel Langhornne Clemens] (1835-1910)

Efficient

Word: Efficient
Word Definition: Being effective with having minimum waste or effort

How you and others can benefit: When someone has the attribute of being efficient at the workplace others will notice that being efficient saves time and energy. If you are not efficient it may lead to rushing through a project or daily tasks, which can result in mistakes.

Past experience about the word: To complete your work in a proficient manner coincides with time management. Also, being detailed oriented will help eliminate any common mistakes.

Tips: It takes less time to do something correctly than it does to correct the problem two or more times. Plan before you act, then act out your plan. This will reduce the amount of times it takes to accomplish a task or project.

Date for applying your change?

What personally has to happen for change to occur?

Two weeks after the change occurred; what changes happened at the workplace and in your personal life?

The most difficult thing in the world is to know how to do a thing and to watch somebody else doing it wrong, without comment.
T. H. White

Focused

Word: Focused
Word Definition: Keeping ones mind set on a particular task, project, career or personal life until they have obtained the results they needed.

How you and others can benefit: By not loosing focus of your responsibilities whether it is at the workplace, home or on a personal level. When you have a responsibility at the workplace, home, or in your personal life it needs to be accomplished in the time frame that has been agreed upon. In some cases sooner could be beneficial. When a person looses sight (focus) it could end up be devastating for the coworkers, clients, friend and family members who are depending on that task to be accomplished. Sometimes, the other associates workload depends on you getting them the needed information or completing your assignment.

Past experience about the word: I can remember when I was working for a company and every day the same person would come into my office and would begin talking to me about things that were not associated with work. Usually, they would stay in my office up to an hour, which would cause me to stay extra hours to complete my work. I started to realize that I would lose my focus on my work. The next time that person came to talk to me I suggested that we meet for lunch once a week so we could talk.

Tips: Losing focus can cost you time, money, employment, family and friends. It is best to be honest with others when needed so you can stay focused.

Date for applying your change?

What personally has to happen for a change to occur?

Two weeks after the change occurred; what changes happened at the workplace and in your personal life?

"If A equals success, then the formula is A equals X plus Y and Z, with X being work, Y play, and Z keeping your mouth shut."
Albert Einstein

<u>Stability</u>

Word: Stability
Word Definition: Resisting sudden change

How you and others can benefit: What an attribute; knowing that someone is stable at their workplace or in their personal life. When a decision is being made by someone who has stability, others know that they will not waiver on their decision.

Past experience about the word: When I have worked with individuals that have this trait, I have noticed that they also have pride in the way they conduct their daily business.

Tips: Stability can be a good trait as well as a weak trait. We have to determine whether we are stable because of complacency or are we afraid of change. Sometimes change can bring that needed growth and that growth can be used to help others.

Date for applying your change?

What personally has to happen for change to occur?

Two weeks after the change occurred; what changes happened at the workplace and in your personal life?

Let no man presume to give advice to others that has not first given council to himself.
Seneca

Body Language

Understanding body language can be an effective tool to help you understand clients, co-workers, friends, family members and your own feelings in situations. Monitoring your own body language can also help put others at ease.

Being argumentative:
Interrupting
Tapping their fingers
Tapping their feet

Being in agreement:
Hands flat on a table
Putting a pen or pencil down

Understanding body language can help you to interpret the clients, co-workers, friends and family member's mood, and how to work with a situation more effectively. This will help determine which approach to take in various circumstances.

NOTES

NOTES

About Scott Godfrey

Scott Godfrey lives with his wife Tracey an her son Averey and their two Jack Russells Buddi and Baxter in Littlestown, Pennsylvania. In the last 30 years he has strived toward educating people in achieving customer satisfaction in different areas. Working with homebuilders, retail stores and many other businesses; educating them on customer service and educating their staff on setting and obtaining expectations for the customer. Godfrey also possesses a real estate license in PA, MD, and VA.

Godfrey has conducted seminars on obtaining customer satisfaction from the unsatisfied customer and worked with businesses to increase productivity as well to make one aware of their daily responsibilities at the workplace. In the past, he has managed the warranty and quality department for a national home builder in the Northern Virginia area. I want to thank Tracey my wife for her devotion, encouragement, understanding and expressing her positive influence while this book was being written.

Godfrey is donating 20 percent of the profits from this book and seminars to Feed the Children, an association that helps feed children and parents in a time of need.

For seminars and speaking engagements, please contact 717-339-9977

978-0-595-48064-7
0-595-48064-0

www.ingramcontent.com/pod-product-compliance
Lightning Source LLC
Chambersburg PA
CBHW051253050326
40689CB00007B/1176